100 THINGS TO DO IN OKLAHOMA CITY BEFORE YOU DIE

3rd Edition

Pumpkinville at Myriad Gardens,
courtesy of Dennis Spielman

100 THINGS TO DO IN OKLAHOMA CITY BEFORE YOU DIE

3rd Edition

JEFF PROVINE AND DENNIS SPIELMAN

REEDY PRESS

Reedy Press
PO Box 5131
St. Louis, MO 63139, USA
reedypress.com

Library of Congress Control Number: 2024939003

ISBN: 9781681065397

Design by Jill Halpin

Printed in the United States of America
24 25 26 27 28   5 4 3 2 1

DEDICATION

To everyone who thinks Oklahoma is a flyover state,
the joke is on you.

FRIDA Southwest, courtesy of Dennis Spielman

CONTENTS

Music and Entertainment

Culture and History

Shopping and Fashion

ACKNOWLEDGMENTS

Dennis would like to thank everyone who shared their story with him for *Uncovering Oklahoma* and those who joined him on his filming adventures.

Jeff would like to thank everyone putting in effort to make OKC a place quite unlike anywhere in the world.

PREFACE

For this third edition of *100 Things to Do in Oklahoma City Before You Die*, we're taking the road less traveled. Everybody knows about Cattlemen's and Pops, and for good reason. Cattlemen's has been serving up steaks in Stockyards City for over a century, and Pops never ceases to amaze as a Route 66 icon with untold varieties of pops (or "cokes" if you're from a bit more to the south). Go to a Thunder game for one of the loudest experiences in the NBA. Visit the Oklahoma City Bombing Memorial in reverence and learn more at our nationally ranked Memorial Museum. Then, we have 100 more things that you may not think of when you think "OKC," which will blow you away just as the wind comes sweeping down the plain.

Oklahoma City has boomed in the past decade. Lower cost of living and a healthy demand for our exports in the 2010s added more than 100,000 people to the population, new towers downtown, and plenty of opportunity for experimentation in restaurants and destinations for tourists and locals alike.

It's not an easy task to trim the list down to only 100 must-do suggestions for the city. As a testament to the city's growth, we challenged ourselves to stick strictly to Oklahoma City limits. There are even more things to check out in the surrounding metropolitan area including Norman, Edmond, Midwest City, and the smaller towns around. Go on a musical adventure in the UCO Jazz Lab, see how we monitor storms at the National Weather Center, and be awed by the lights at Christmas in the

Park in Yukon. If we could include them all, we might be looking at 1,000 or more Things to Do.

For our 100 list, we've assembled the coolest of the cool in categories for eats, experiences, and shopping. Food alone could easily be its own 100 list, and there are constantly new venues and trucks people should give a try. Some of our things are actually their own sublists to show where to get the weirdest art, best records, or unexpected gifts. We'll keep everyone informed on new places, too, with #100okctodo and #UncoveringOklahoma.

There's always a new adventure to be had. Here's a list of great places to get started.

Cafe Kacao, courtesy of Dennis Spielman

FOOD AND DRINK

1

"COME THRU"
TO MA DER LAO KITCHEN

Ma Der Lao Kitchen is not just a dining experience; it's a journey into the heart of Lao culinary traditions, where each bite tells a story of Executive Chef Jeff Chanchaleune's family. Lao cuisine is similar to Thai food but focuses on savory and spicy elements, and sticky rice is essential to the Lao dining experience. The menu showcases a variety of dishes, including the chuen gai (twice-fried chicken) and the house-made sai oua (Lao sausage) with its 20-ingredient blend of herbs and spices. The jaew bong, a red roasted chili dip, adds a bold kick to the meal.

Ma Der Lao Kitchen collaborates with Lively Beerworks to create a rice lager that perfectly balances the spiciness of the dishes with its light, crisp, and flavorful profile. The restaurant offers vegan alternatives and creates an inviting atmosphere with "no wrong way to eat Lao food."

1634 N Blackwelder Ave., Ste.102, 405-900-5503
maderlaokitchen.com

2

BRUNCH
AT CAFE KACAO

If you are looking for an exceptional brunch experience, Cafe Kacao is a must to try: this family-owned Guatemalan restaurant is one of the most popular spots in the city. The menu features a variety of Latin-inspired dishes from different countries such as El Salvador, Mexico, and Brazil. In addition to their delicious food, they have a full-service espresso bar that offers innovative drinks, including the famous orange zest mocha and the refreshing iced horchata latte. It's worth noting that the portion sizes are quite generous, so it might be a good idea to share an appetizer like the pupusas and an entrée if it's your first time there. Every dish at Cafe Kacao is bursting with Guatemalan flavors, making it a destination for anyone who wants to experience authentic cuisine.

3325 N Classen Blvd., 405-584-6361
cafekacao.com

TIP

Arrive early to avoid long waits. The café closes by midafternoon, so people are eager to get inside!

3

WINE DOWN
AT THE STUDY

The Study prides itself on its approachable take on wine, highlighting that "at its core, it's just fermented grape juice." While owner Ian Bennett has a deep passion for wine, he has created a space where anyone can relax and enjoy a glass in an unpretentious atmosphere. The interior design is cozy and reminiscent of a house, with different rooms to explore as well as outdoor seating.

With a selection of more than 60 wines on tap, The Study has something for everyone, whether it be a familiar or unique wine. Patrons can explore various options and enjoy multiple pour sizes, allowing them to try new wines without breaking the bank.

Whether you're a seasoned wine enthusiast or just starting to explore the world of wine, The Study welcomes you to embark on a comfortable and enjoyable wine journey.

701 W Sheridan Ave., Ste. 100, 405-724-7514
thestudyokc.com

4

HOP ON
THE CRAFT BEER TRAIL

Oklahoma's brewery taprooms may be a relatively new addition since their legalization in 2016, but the state is quickly making up for lost time with a range of quality offerings. With more than a dozen breweries operating in the city, the best way to explore them is with a Craft Beer Trail passport from the Craft Brewers Association of Oklahoma. This not-for-profit organization is committed to strengthening and unifying the Oklahoma brewing industry, and its mobile-exclusive passport is a collection of carefully curated craft beer locations that offer free full-pour samples.

The best part? Your passport will be instantly delivered to your phone via text and email, ready to use immediately. There's no need to download an app, and you can save your pass to your phone's home screen for easy, one-tap access. When you visit a participating business, all you have to do is show your pass to an attendant or staff member to redeem your offering.

craftbeerok.org

THE CRAFT BEER TRAIL

Angry Scotsman Brewing
704 W Reno Ave., 405-673-7713
angryscotbrew.com

Anthem Brewing
908 SW 4th St., 405-604-0446
anthembrewing.com

Bricktown Brewery
1 N Oklahoma Ave., 405-232-2739
bricktownbrewery.com

Broke Brewing Co.
3810 N Tulsa Ave., Ste. Z, 405-237-8115
broke.beer

Coop Ale Works
4745 Council Heights Rd., 405-842-2667
coopaleworks.com

Core4 Brewing Company
7 N Lee Ave., 405-215-9671
core4brewing.com

Fair-Weather Friend
314 N Klein Ave., 405-215-9081
fwfbeer.com

Lively Beerworks
815 SW 2nd St., 405-594-8100
livelybeerworks.com

MadHopper Brewing
923 W Britton Ave., 419-450-2434
madhopperbrewing.beer

Oklahoma Craft Nano Brewhouse Kitchen and Coffee
12 E California Ave., 405-768-4416
oklacraft.com

OK Cider Co.
705 W Sheridan Ave., 405-501-8877
okciderco.com

Prairie Artisan Ales
3 NE 8th St., 405-602-0894
prairieales.com

Roughtail Brewing Company
320 W Memorial Rd., 405-771-6517
roughtailbeer.com

Skydance Brewing Company
1 NE 7th St., Ste. A, 405-768-2154
skydancebrewing.com

Stonecloud Brewing Company
1012 NW 1st St., Ste. 101, 405-602-3966
stonecloudbrewing.com

The Big Friendly
1737 Spoke St., 405-492-3785
thebigfriendly.com

Vanessa House Beer Co.
118 NW 8th St., 405-724-9330
vanessahousebeerco.com

EAT A TACO AS BIG AS A MACHETE
AT SUPER TORTAS EL CHAVO

The story behind Super Tortas El Chavo is a family affair, with the owner's father having grown up watching the beloved Mexican character El Chavo. The restaurant's name is a nod to this cultural icon, and the family's dedication to providing an authentic experience shines through in every dish. While this Mexican restaurant is known for its tortas, among its standout creations is the Machete Taco. This oversized taco, reminiscent of a machete knife, features a generous helping of meat, lettuce, tomato, onion, avocado, sour cream, and a sprinkle of cheese. The signature dish is wrapped in their freshly made corn masa and represents the family's passion for sharing the best of Mexican cuisine with their community. Bring a friend if you go for a machete or a torta, since they are hearty meals.

721 SW 29th St., 405-631-0100
supertortaselchavook.com

BE BOLD
AT FRIDA SOUTHWEST

FRIDA Southwest makes you feel like you left OKC and stepped into Santa Fe by blending the vibrant spirit of Frida Kahlo with the rich flavors of American and Southwestern cuisine. Executive Chef Quinn Carroll, the mastermind behind the menu, takes pride in crafting dishes that encapsulate the diverse culinary influences, offering a fusion of Mexican, Southern comfort, and Southwestern vibes. The food menu doesn't just cater to carnivores; it's a testament to inclusivity with an array of vegan options. The innovative heart of palm "calamari," a vegan twist on a classic favorite, showcases FRIDA's dedication to accommodating various dietary preferences without compromising flavor.

In addition to its exceptional food and lively atmosphere, FRIDA has a hidden speakeasy called The Daley, a cozy hideaway with bookshelves filled with art and design books.

500 Paseo, 405-683-7432
fridasouthwest.com

BREAK GROUP INDECISIVENESS BY EATING AT A FOOD HALL

Have you ever been in a situation where you're trying to organize a dinner or lunch with friends, but everyone has different preferences when it comes to food, and some people may arrive later than others? Finding a place that accommodates everyone's needs and preferences can be challenging, not to mention the added headache of splitting the check. Thankfully, there are not one but two solutions: The Collective and Parlor OKC. These two food halls feature multiple restaurant concepts under one roof, so everyone can choose what they want and join the group for a shared meal. Food choices range from tacos to Philly cheesesteaks to Hawaiian to Korean fusion to pizza and more.

Both venues have a bar and patio seating, so picking between the two boils down to what food concepts you think everyone will enjoy more, but both are great choices.

The Collective
308 NW 10th St.
thecollectiveokc.com

The Parlor OKC
11 NE 6th St.
parlorokc.com

8

TRAVEL A WORLD OF FLAVORS
AT BLACK WALNUT AND GREY SWEATER

Helmed by Chef Andrew Black, crowned the 2023 James Beard Best Chef Southwest, Black Walnut is a culinary gem where eclectic flavors meet an unpretentious ambiance. The menu reflects a thoughtful fusion of diverse tastes, perfectly balancing upscale dining and a relaxed, welcoming atmosphere. Try the famed Tomahawk Steak, and you'll rave, too.

Adjacent to Black Walnut is its sister concept, Grey Sweater, which offers a different experience with a tiered tasting menu that showcases the most unique and unforgettable flavors from around the world. Instead of a set menu, the staff at Grey Sweater interviews guests during the reservation process to offer a personalized culinary journey. In addition to a curated wine menu, they were the first in Oklahoma to have a water menu with a selection of still and sparkling waters from around the world.

100 NE 4th St.

Black Walnut
405-445-6273
blackwalnutokc.com

Grey Sweater
405-445-6274
greysweaterokc.com

9

SHUCK
AT SEDALIA'S OYSTER & SEAFOOD

Sedalia's Oyster & Seafood stands out from the rest with their commitment to culinary innovation. They frequently update their menu, ensuring that their oysters, crudos, and grilled dishes constantly evolve. Co-owner and Executive Chef Zach Walters emphasizes that "we put a lot of time and care into making sure that all the dishes on the menu are unique, that they have their own story and characteristics."

Apart from their seafood offerings, Sedalia's also prides itself on providing an excellent wine experience. Their curated wine list encourages guests to explore and indulge in their thoughtfully selected wines. With their ever-changing menu, innovative dishes, and dedication to pushing boundaries, Sedalia's has carved a niche in the city's dynamic dining scene. If you're a seafood enthusiast with an adventurous palate, Sedalia's is the place to be.

2727 NW 10th St., 405-626-8249
sedaliasokc.com

TIP

Due to the intimate nature of their location, reservations are encouraged.

10

TRY VIETNAMESE FUSION
AT RIVIÈRE MODERN BÁNH MÌ

Rivière Modern Bánh Mì is a trendy restaurant and bar located in the Midtown district known for its culinary fusion in Vietnamese cuisine. They specialize in crafting gourmet banh mi sandwiches and a diverse array of Asian delights. While they do not strictly adhere to tradition, their expert blend of modern and classic flavors promises a delightful dining experience.

For an authentic Vietnamese treat, indulge in their Vietnamese pho. This dish features scratch-made pho broth along with rice noodles, thinly sliced steak, braised brisket, sliced white onion, scallion, and cilantro. The stars of the menu are their banh mi options. For a playful twist, try the banh mi tacos, which are available with corn or flour tortillas. These tacos are adorned with pickled carrot, jalapeño, cucumber, cilantro, and sriracha aioli and come with a choice of protein. They are a delightful fusion of Vietnamese and Mexican influences.

905 N Hudson Ave., 405-604-3446
rivièreokc.com

TIP

Their burgers are chef's-kiss good.

DON'T BE AFRAID
OF GHST

Indulge in the vibrant allure of GHST Restaurant & Bar, a culinary gem located in the lively Midtown district. This chic restaurant impresses its guests with its craft cocktails and delicious cuisine, creating a sophisticated atmosphere that attracts both locals and visitors.

GHST is a haven for those who crave a fusion of exquisite flavors and top-notch service. The skilled team is committed to culinary excellence and creates daily delights, ensuring that every dish is a testament to their passion for quality, from caprese gushers to steak frites poutine. Executive Chef Zach Hutton, a James Beard Award nominee, leads the team. The menu at GHST offers a diverse symphony of flavors, promising a gastronomic journey that caters to every palate.

805 N Hudson Ave., 405-493-9560
ghstokc.com

12

SHARE
AT RISERVA BAR + TAPAS

At Riserva Bar + Tapas, sharing is not just a practice; it's an art form. Every item on the menu is meant to be savored collectively, encouraging diners to master the delightful experience of communal dining. Riserva crafts globally inspired, shareable plates using only the finest ingredients, from freshly ground spices to organic produce. Chef James Fox, drawing on his extensive travel and educational experiences, skillfully combines flavors from around the world to deliver bright and robust creations. The restaurant also offers a carefully curated beverage program that includes uniquely inspired craft cocktails and hand-selected wines from Spain, the Mediterranean, and beyond, ensuring a perfect pairing for every palate. Bring a group of friends for the best shareable experience.

1332 W Memorial Ave., Ste. 108, 405-286-2476
riservatapas.com

HAVE A SLICE
AT EMPIRE SLICE HOUSE

There's the never-ending debate about who has the best pizza in Oklahoma City. It often comes down to personal taste or the style of pizza, whether deep dish, crispy thin crust, square Detroit, and on and on. No list of top pizza places is complete without Empire Slice, whose New York–style slices have been thrilling OKC taste buds since 2013. The trick to eating it is to fold midway in the crust, letting all the toppings come together in food heaven.

Empire Slice follows the motto "Live Free, Pie Hard." Their Plaza District eatery's easygoing atmosphere is spreading all around town with "Slice Shop" counters. True to New York form, there are daily slice specials, and the creativity is all original. Check out the Joezilla featuring barbecue sriracha sauce, the blue cheese Rocksteady, or the Ghostface Killah with ghost chili marinara. And if you've never had an artichoke dip, prepare to be blown away.

1804 NW 16th St., 405-557-1760
empireslicepizza.com

TIP

Check out the Slice Shops around town for a quick bite from counter service. You'll find them in Nichols Hills at 1125 NW 63rd St., Mayfair Village at 4723 N May Ave., and in the Paycom Center.

FAMILY MATTERS
AT LA COCINA DE DOÑA NENA

La Cocina de Doña Nena holds a special place in the hearts of its patrons, thanks to the culinary legacy of Doña Nena herself. Doña Nena's culinary prowess, passed down through generations, infuses every dish with a magical touch. From handmade tortillas to some of the best barbacoa tacos in the city, the menu at La Cocina de Doña Nena celebrates authenticity and tradition. The restaurant effortlessly transports diners to the vibrant streets of Chalchihuites, Zacatecas, where the family's journey began.

Family and culture are the pillars of La Cocina de Doña Nena. Sergio and Rosa, Doña Nena's children, have brought their hometown's authentic flavors to Oklahoma City, sharing their family's journey from Mexico. For those seeking an authentic Mexican dining experience beyond expectations, La Cocina de Doña Nena is a must-visit destination.

3710 S May Ave., 405-605-2600

TIP

Elevate your dining experience by pairing your meal with a refreshing agua fresca. Opt for flavors like melon or tamarind to complement the richness of the dishes.

15

RISE

FOR HARVEY BAKERY & KITCHEN

For those who love carbs, Harvey Bakery & Kitchen is the perfect destination. They offer an amazing range of pastries that are flakier than even the most critical croissant connoisseur's expectations. Additionally, their coffee selection is impressive and will wake you up in a snap. The bakery's menu includes various types of bread, pastries, and sweets such as croissants, absolute fudge cookies, Oklahoma sourdough, and caramel morning buns. There are gluten-free and vegan options, including cinnamon rolls, too, available for those with dietary restrictions. Plus, with the monthly specials by Chef Alyssa Ulrich, the offerings will never be stale.

For a bakery, the lobby can accommodate an impressive amount of people, and that's not including their outdoor patio. If you're looking for a place to host a group, the upstairs library is a bright, cozy historic getaway.

301 NW 13th St., 405-898-8811
theharveybakery.com

TIP

Visit their website for their daily bread schedule, croissant of the month, and latte of the month.

16

UNWIND
AT GANACHE PATISSERIE

Ganache Patisserie stands out in the world of bakeries, specializing in a delectable array of French and Italian pastries, breads, desserts, and brunch items. What distinguishes Ganache is its unwavering commitment to quality and authenticity. Started by husband and wife Laura Szyld and Matt Ruggi, they elevate the culinary experience by exclusively using premium European ingredients, resulting in a flavor profile that sets them apart by being distinctly less sweet than other establishments.

The bakery's emphasis on small batches is a testament to their dedication to freshness and meticulous attention to detail. However, because of the nature of their smaller batches, if you need a bunch of goodies for a party, you may want to order a few days in advance. While you're there, grab yourself a drink from the extensive coffee and tea menu to complete your sensory delight.

13230 Pawnee Dr., Ste. 114, 405-286-4068
ganacheokc.com

TIP

Ganache Patisserie has one of the best hot chocolates in the city. They serve you a cup filled with chocolate shavings, and then they pour the hot milk in front of you and top off with whipped cream.

17

YAM
ABOUT FLORENCE'S RESTAURANT

Florence's Restaurant is not just a local favorite; it's also gained national attention for its clever homestyle cooking. It has left its mark on the foodie map after being featured on *Diners, Drive-Ins and Dives* and was the first restaurant in Oklahoma City to win the prestigious James Beard Award.

The restaurant dates back to 1952 when Mrs. Florence Jones Kemp founded it at the young age of 20. Today, the restaurant still stands and continues to serve its customers. The star of its menu is the delectable Yammed Fried Chicken, which combines the crispy goodness of fried chicken with the unique flavor of one of their most popular vegetables. Diners can indulge in this delight, accompanied by a choice of three vegetables or two vegetables and a Nice Little Salad.

1437 NE 23rd St., 405-427-3663
theflorencesrestaurant.com

PUSH THE MOON
TO ACCESS LUNAR LOUNGE

You don't need Mulder and Scully's assistance to find this hidden speakeasy, but you do need some special directions. However, be warned that it's not a simple walk-up to this speakeasy. You'll need to channel your inner Fox Mulder and use your investigative skills to find the entrance.

Go to the Midtown Plaza Court building and search for a door that will bring you closer to the truth. The most accessible entrance is on the west side, between businesses. Once you're inside, look for a crescent moon button to open the hidden entrance. This space-and-sci-fi-themed speakeasy will make you feel like you're on an extraterrestrial adventure. The cocktails are simply out of this world—they may even convince you that the truth is still out there!

1114 Classen Dr.
lunarloungeokc.com

SIP AWAY TO A TROPICAL PARADISE

AT FLAMINGO TIKI

The unmistakable pink building of Flamingo Tiki beckons cocktail enthusiasts and seekers of vibrant atmospheres, proving you don't need to go to the beach to enjoy a tropical setting. Whether it's your first visit or you're a regular, the lively, tropical ambiance will make your experience memorable every time you come. Hungry patrons can complement their drinks with a limited menu from Oso, the sister Mexican restaurant.

The Flamingo cocktail, named after the bar, is a fan favorite and top seller. Crafted with the exclusive pink pineapple, this secret recipe concoction blends various rums, grenadine, hibiscus, and a touch of sparkling wine. The result? A visually stunning and delectable Tiki masterpiece that captures the essence of the exotic.

With its imaginative drinks, tropical vibes, and welcoming patio, this tiki bar is a testament to Humankind Hospitality's commitment to creating unique and unforgettable spaces in Oklahoma City.

605 NW 28th St., 405-309-8226
osopaseo.com/flamingo-tiki-room

TIP

For the devoted regulars, ask about the Passport Program. Explore a curated selection of Tiki concoctions, collect stamps, and upon completion, become eligible for exciting prizes. It's a journey that rewards those who fully embrace the Tiki spirit.

20

EAT WITH THE WINNERS
AT BIG TRUCK TACOS

There's nothing like a taco truck, and there's nobody like Big Truck Tacos. They had their start on a rolling kitchen serving creations inspired by Mexican street food, which was such a hit they were voted America's Favorite Food Truck on Food Network. The trucks still cater, but now most people come to its stationary restaurant.

The Big Truck menu is packed with tasty options. The tacos are straightforward deliciousness, like the Chicken Tinga being chicken tinga with onions and some cilantro. Others have more stylized names, like the Flaming Lips commemorative taco with smoked tongue, pico, avocado, and queso fresco. Then there's the famous 5th Amendment with ingredients they're not at liberty to divulge! Tacos are only the start, of course, with burritos, flautas, and a chicken tortilla soup so good it has prompted road trips of hundreds of miles just for a bowl.

530 NW 23rd St., 405-525-8226
bigtrucktacos.com

TIP

Big Truck offers some of the best vegetarian options in the city. Plenty of tacos and burritos are vegetarian to begin with, and there is always the option for tofu as your protein of choice.

21

WING OVER
TO CARICAN FLAVORS

With a warm sense of community, Carican Flavors combines cultural and culinary traditions with health-conscious choices. Their authentic Jamaican jerk seasoning their chicken is a true delight. For those seeking a break from meat-centric dishes, the menu offers vegetarian treats that redefine the perception of Caribbean cuisine. The restaurant became a certified healthy establishment, recognizing the diverse dietary needs of its patrons. Sharon McMillan, the owner, is passionate about making better choices and actively engages with customers to ensure they make informed and health-conscious decisions.

Apart from its delicious food, Carican Flavors boasts a selection of fresh juices that go beyond mere refreshment. These juices are crafted to address specific health concerns and are rooted in a holistic approach to well-being. Each concoction serves as a medicinal elixir, from boosting immunity to aiding digestion.

2701 N Martin Luther King Ave., 405-424-0456
caricanflavors.com

3.14 YOURSELF
TO PIE JUNKIE

From the hand-rolled crusts to the gooey fillings, every element at Pie Junkie is crafted with care, embodying the spirit of homemade goodness. What started as a casual collaboration has evolved into a thriving business that continues to delight pie enthusiasts with its delectable creations.

Pie Junkie stands out not only for the deliciousness of their pies but also for the genuine love and dedication that goes into each one. Their menu features a range of flavors, including signature pies like Drunken Turtle and Peanut Butter Chocolate, as well as cream pies like Coconut Cream and French Silk. The selection of pies is a perfect blend of classic favorites and innovative combinations, catering to a diverse range of tastes. In addition to pies by the slice, you can order six-inch cutie pies, whole pies, frozen take-and-bake meals, quiche, and whoopie pies by the dozen.

1711 NW 16th St., 405-605-8767
piejunkie.com

23

PET THE CATS
AT DON'T STRESS MEOWT

OKC's cat café champions live by three simple words: coffee, cats, and cuddles. Operating in partnership with Safe Haven Animal Rescue, the café offers a glass-enclosed "Cat Lounge" where 15 to 25 adoptable kitties can come out to play, crossing a sky bridge over the hallway from their litter boxes and resting area. Guests book their visits to the Cat Lounge in advance and can even host whole parties with up to 20 people hanging out on comfy chairs, petting kitties, and, most importantly, handing out treats.

Beyond the Cat Lounge, patrons can still watch the cats through the wall while they enjoy the café, no reservation needed. The café shop offers cat-themed gifts along with frosted specialty cookies and coffees bearing clever names. Have a sip of "espurrso," a "catpuccino," or seasonal drinks that are limited time only.

1900 Linwood Blvd., Ste. 300
dontstressmeowt-catcafe.com/okc

TAKE ARTFUL BITES
AT PICASSO CAFE

Known for its diverse menu and commitment to accommodating various dietary preferences, Picasso Cafe is a true reflection of the vibrant and eclectic atmosphere of the Paseo Arts District. With the building having a long history as a restaurant, the menu at Picasso Cafe has transitioned to include an extensive array of vegetarian and plant-based options, catering to the evolving preferences of the community. Their food inclusivity extends beyond human diners, offering a dog-friendly patio and a dedicated Doggy Dining menu. From chicken risotto to puppuccinos, Picasso ensures everyone, including our four-legged friends, can enjoy the dining experience. Whether you're a vegan enthusiast, a meat lover, or dining with your furry friend, Picasso Cafe has something for everyone.

3009 Paseo Dr., 405-602-2002
picassosonpaseo.com

TIP

For those seeking a quieter dining experience or hoping to catch happy-hour deals, the adjacent sister bar, the Other Room, serves the entire menu from Picasso Cafe, in addition to their own cocktail menu.

DRINK SUSTAINABLE BEANS
AT CLARITY COFFEE

Many people don't think about where their coffee comes from, but at Clarity Coffee, it's right on the bag. The origin of your drink is just the beginning, as Clarity will explain the processing, roasting, and even the method of brewing. Prefer the smooth flow of a Chemex, the pressing of a Prismo, or the crust-cracking Clever dripper? These are subtleties that you may miss until you're in the know.

While you enjoy your brew, also pick up a cookie, scone, danish, or fritter. A coffee alone may be nice, but your palate will thank you as you switch from one deliciousness to the next, staying fresh with every bite or sip. Also take a delightful look through the art galleries stocked by local artists, making each visit to Clarity truly eye-opening to the possibilities.

431 W Main St., Ste. A
1801 Wheeler St., Ste. 170
claritycoffee.com

MORE GREAT COFFEE SPOTS IN OKC

Elemental Coffee
815 N Hudson Ave., 405-633-1703
elementalcoffee.com

Holey Rollers
3010 Paseo, Ste. 101, 405-212-2383
holeyrollersdonuts.com

Junction Coffee
611 N Broadway Ave., 405-252-1148
junctioncoffeeokc.com

Kaiser's Grateful Bean Cafe
1039 N Walker Ave., 405-236-3503
kaisersgratefulbean.com

Perets Coffee Bar
701 W Sheridan Ave.
peretscoffee.com

The Red Cup
3122 N Classen Blvd., 405-525-3430
theredcupokc.com

Sincerely Coffee Roasters
1325 N Walker Ave., Ste. 134
sincerely.coffee

Toast & Coffee
2416 N Robinson Ave., 405-778-6294
toastandcoffeeokc.com

Woodshed Coffee & Tea
7518 N May Ave., 405-563-7213
woodshedtea.com

EAT AT THE TOP OF OKC
AT VAST

Oklahoma is famous for being able to see to the distant horizon, and it's all the easier at the top of the city's tallest skyscraper. Forty-nine stories up the Devon Tower, guests can see upwards of 50 miles on a clear day, whether to the grain elevators of Shawnee and Chickasha or nearly to the OSU campus in Stillwater. Why not have a bite to eat while you're there?

The locally inspired, locally sourced menus at Vast change weekly with regular favorites like an obligatory Oklahoma steak as well as seasonal dishes including strozzapreti pasta. If patrons are only needing a nibble, they can grab some bar food such as hand-cut garlic fries or go straight to dessert like a crème brûlée or tart. There are also plenty of grown-up drinks to sip, from international fare to the famed Neon Sunshine from OKC's own Stonecloud Brewing Company.

333 W Sheridan Ave., 49th floor, 405-702-7262
vastokc.com

TIP

Dinners can be pretty pricey, but lunch buffets are much easier on the wallet at only $25.50 per person ($12.75 for children 12 and under). This includes unlimited house-made desserts!

27

EMBARK ON PURE PERFECTION

AT ZERO TOLERANCE COFFEE AND CHOCOLATE

Zero Tolerance Coffee and Chocolate offers coffee and chocolate made directly from the bean. Their meticulous operation process transforms raw cacao beans into the shiny, mouthwatering chocolate bars patrons have come to adore. This journey starts with sourcing only the finest cacao pods from rainforest belts worldwide, ensuring the best possible taste and reflecting their dedication to ethical farming practices.

Owners Maura and Roy Baker aim to educate patrons on the true essence of chocolate: unadulterated and pure. So, if you're someone who has zero tolerance for lousy chocolate and coffee, then add Zero Tolerance Coffee and Chocolate to your list. Embark on a sensory journey with them and experience the true essence of chocolate and coffee like never before!

919 W Britton Rd., 405-314-0048
zerotolerancecoffee.com

The Alex Sanchez and Cat Pitt Comedy Experience at Theatre Crude Fringe Festival, courtesy of Dennis Spielman

MUSIC AND ENTERTAINMENT

28

SAY "YES AND . . ."
TO OKC IMPROV

Picture yourself grabbing a drink at the bar and settling into a seat, ready to witness a group of talented individuals creating moments of hilarity on stage based on your suggestions. OKC Improv offers you this experience where the audience becomes part of the magic. Whether it's an improvised musical or a theatrical scene built on the spot, you'll be amazed by the wit and camaraderie of the performers.

What sets OKC Improv apart is not just the laughter-inducing shows but also the opportunity to learn the art of improv through their diverse range of classes. There are classes for everyone, from foundational levels to specialized workshops and sketch comedy classes. The theater's commitment to community goes beyond entertainment, with family-friendly shows, sensory-accessible performances, and outreach programs for Alzheimer's caregivers and veterans. Join them in living life through laughter.

1755 NW 16th St., 405-456-9858
okcimprov.com

29

GET UP CLOSE AND PERSONAL
AT CARPENTER SQUARE THEATRE

As a year-round live theater company, Carpenter Square Theatre's commitment to delivering a diverse range of performances is evident in their repertoire. From award-winning modern works that push the boundaries of storytelling to uproarious comedy classics, one-night-only world premieres, and outlandish musicals that ignite the stage, there's something for every theater enthusiast. What sets this theater apart is its intimate setting, which can accommodate only 120 viewers. This cozy arrangement creates an immersive experience, allowing the audience to connect with the performers on a personal level. You can take a stroll through the art gallery or grab a refreshment from the bar before the show or during intermission to complement your theatrical experience. As the lights dim and the curtains rise, you'll find yourself drawn into the world unfolding before you.

1009 W Reno St., 405-232-6500
carpentersquare.com

LAUGH OUT LOUD
AT BRICKTOWN COMEDY CLUB

Local and national comedians bring the laughs at Bricktown Comedy Club with diverse comedic performances that promise to tickle your funny bone. In addition to the laughs, their menu includes shareables, wraps, sweet treats, and an array of specialty cocktails and mocktails. As with most comedy clubs, they do have a drink and item minimum, but this can be anything off the menu, including food.

Suppose you want to hone your own comedy skills. In that case, the Bricktown Comedy Academy covers the fundamentals of the craft with engaging workshops and hands-on guidance. The culmination is a live performance in front of a receptive audience, allowing you to test your newfound skills and bask in a lively crowd's applause.

409 E California Ave., 405-594-0505
bricktowncomedy.com

TIP

If you're seeking to witness emerging acts and performers bravely testing new material, the perfect nights to visit are New Talent Tuesday or any of their Open Mic Nights.

31

TOUR THE CITY ON A BIKE

WITH RIDE OKC

Founders Ryan and Ashley always liked to book bike tours to cities they visited as an immersive, low-speed way to get to know the ins and outs of their destination. There wasn't much like that in OKC. So, they made it happen!

Now thousands of people have ridden the streets on Ride OKC's many tours. The educational Art + Architecture and City History Tours are just the beginning. The Cookie Tour is particularly exciting for kids and those young at heart as people pedal to some of OKC's best sweet shops. For older riders, the Bikes + Brews Tour hits different breweries and includes a drink at each one. Seasonal special tours take guests on a haunted bike ride in October and a ride-by of the best holiday lights as the Christmas season gets going.

They even offer custom tours for anyone looking for something particular that may not be widely available. That's how you make it happen.

428 W California Ave., 405-309-9696
rideokc.com

THROW DOWN ON THE POTTERY WHEEL

WITH PASEO POTTERY

Unearth your creative side by enrolling in a pottery class at Paseo Pottery. Picture yourself shaping clay while surrounded by the lively atmosphere of Paseo Arts District's eclectic galleries and eateries. Paseo Pottery has a team of skilled instructors who provide a warm and encouraging environment for both beginners and experienced artisans. Their reputation of fine work has several local restaurants, such as FRIDA Southwest, using their pottery for their tableware.

If you are not yet ready to create your own masterpieces or if you are searching for inspiration, you can explore the gallery at Paseo Pottery, which features unique pieces made by local artists available for purchase. This is a great way to adorn your space with unique handcrafted art pieces that are visually stimulating and support the local creative community.

3017 Paseo, 405-525-3017

GIVE A LISTEN
TO THE OKC PHILHARMONIC

For a century, Oklahoma Cityans have been listening to some of the best tunes musicians can offer. The Oklahoma City Symphony started a century ago with its classical repertoire and then-new fare, and today we have the philharmonic continuing the tradition in the Civic Center Music Hall's Thelma Gaylord Performing Arts Theatre. Keep a close eye (or ear) on the Phil's season, where you'll be able to hear classical music dating back centuries, modern creations and interpretations, and Broadway stars coming to join in the musical extravaganza.

Since music is such an expansive topic, the philharmonic offers something for everyone. Die-hard traditionalists will enjoy orchestral classics like Brahms and Liszt. Other folks might be more in tune with a "Pops" concert featuring everything from movie scores to jazz. Popular concerts include sing-alongs to pop and Disney favorites that will turn the audience into performers themselves, sharing in the musical creation.

424 Colcord Dr., Ste. B, 405-842-5387
okcphil.org

34

EXPERIENCE DANCE

WITH THE OKLAHOMA CITY BALLET

"Ballet" might not be the first thing to come to mind when word-associating with "Oklahoma City," but that would be missing out on some of the finest performances in the metro. Going strong for more than 50 years, the Oklahoma City Ballet has been inspiring audiences with dance that is riveting both technically and emotionally. The ballet frequently teams with the Oklahoma City Philharmonic to present a feast for the ears as well as the eyes as they reenact famous, long-lived choreography as well as new productions.

Much of the ballet's attention is dedicated to training up the next generation of great dancers. Classes for folks as young as three years old build on our bodies' natural instincts into movements with technical foundations. Truly outstanding participants are invited to the Studio Company and may even be counted among the world-class Professional Company, rubbing shoulders with dancers from around the globe.

6800 N Classen Blvd., 405-843-9898
okcballet.org

35

SPEND A SUMMERTIME EVENING

WITH THE SUNDAY TWILIGHT CONCERT SERIES

Get ready to rock out and roll over to the Myriad Botanical Gardens, where the Sunday Twilight Concert Series is in full swing! This free outdoor concert is the perfect way to jazz up your summer evenings. The Arts Council Oklahoma City has curated an eclectic mix of bands that will have you tapping your feet and bobbing your head. With genres that range from blues to funk and everything in between, there's something for every music lover. The Devon Lawn is where all the action takes place, so don't be a solo act—bring your friends and family along for a harmonic experience. And remember to pack your cooler with snacks and drinks to keep you fueled up throughout the night. Come on down and groove to the beat under the stars!

400 W California Ave., 405-270-4848
artscouncilokc.com

TWIRL IN THE SKY
WITH PERPETUAL MOTION DANCE

Perpetual Motion Dance, a beacon of innovation in movement, creates performances that defy both gravity and expectations. For over two decades, they have mesmerized audiences with their unique fusion of postmodern and aerial techniques, executed with a signature blend of grace and technical brilliance that leaves viewers in a state of wonder.

Perpetual Motion Dance is more than just a stage performance—it's an invitation to experience the extraordinary. With classes that explore the ethereal realms of aerial dance, including captivating silk routines, they extend a warm welcome to enthusiasts of all levels, encouraging them to reach new heights. Their artistry is a reminder that the human spirit is capable of incredible things, and their dedication to their craft inspires all. Whether you choose to take a class or witness a performance, let Perpetual Motion Dance ignite a spark of inspiration and elevate your soul's flight.

405-283-6852
perpetualmotiondance.org

37

ATTEND BROADWAY IN OKC
AT LYRIC THEATRE

With beginnings from the Kirkpatrick Fine Arts Auditorium at Oklahoma City University in 1963 to the opening of their own venue in 2007 that served as a catalyst for the revitalization of the historic Plaza District, Lyric Theatre of Oklahoma is a nationally recognized, Broadway-caliber theater. Lyric's *A Christmas Carol* has become a holiday tradition.

But wait, there's more! Lyric Theatre is not content with just dazzling adults; they've got a whole bag of tricks for the little ones, too. Enter the Thelma Gaylord Academy, where the spotlight shines on budding talents through classes and private lessons. Lyric Theatre also takes the show on the road with its Musical Interactive program, hitting schools across the state like a traveling carnival of melody and rhythm.

1727 NW 16th St., 405-524-9312
lyrictheatreokc.com

GET THEE
TO OKLAHOMA SHAKESPEARE IN THE PARK

Since 1985, Oklahoma City has been treated to classics by the Bard in the open air, about as close to the original thing as people can get today. As the heat of the day subsides to the cool of the evening, the crowd gathers, bringing with them their seating choices of folding chairs or picnic blankets. Their mouths enjoy snacks and drinks, but it is their eyes and ears that are truly in for a delectable feast as art that has stood time's test for centuries comes to life once again.

Today Oklahoma Shakespeare in the Park is going strong with several plays each season as well as shows from other authors in the canon like Austen and Dickens. As a Tier I Small Professional Theatre and in accordance with the Actors' Equity Association, Oklahoma Shakespeare brings top-notch acting craft to OKC for jaw-dropping performances.

2920 Paseo, 405-235-3700
okshakes.org

TIP

Shakespeare in the Park also holds productions indoors during the chillier months in their Black Box Theatre, an intimate space for audiences of up to 55.

39

RALLY
WITH OKC REP

Oklahoma City Repertory Theater is a nonprofit organization dedicated to championing new ways of making theater, supporting innovative artists, and growing Oklahoma City's cultural ecology. With a mission to provide quality theater experiences for the community, OKC REP is committed to bringing diverse stories to life onstage and fostering an environment of creativity and collaboration.

Located in the heart of downtown Oklahoma City, OKC REP makes its home at Oklahoma Contemporary's Te Ata Theater, which provides an intimate setting for a deeply immersive experience between the audience and the performers. Each season, OKC REP presents a variety of productions ranging from classic plays to modern works, with a focus on small-cast plays that often feature performers from Oklahoma and around the world. Be sure to arrive early for their preshow ritual REP Rallies, where before they open up the theater, a local artist takes over for a magical moment that can include everything from song, dance, poetry, comedy, drag shows, and genre-defying moments.

405-768-2191
okcrep.org

40

GO OFFSTAGE
WITH SOUTHERN PLAINS PRODUCTIONS

Southern Plains Productions offers a unique and innovative approach to theater by creating site-specific stories that engage audiences in nontraditional locations. Although they do not have a permanent theater space, they utilize Oklahoma City's diverse range of venues to create a one-of-a-kind theater experience. For instance, their production of *Silent Sky* was presented in the planetarium of Science Museum Oklahoma, featuring an actress proficient in sign language. For *The Chinese Lady*, they transformed the back of a retail space into an art museum.

If you're interested in theater, the Studio offers virtual classes in storytelling, performance, directing, and even the business side of theater. Southern Plains Productions aims to reimagine live theater with innovative artistic experiences that spark conversations and unite the Oklahoma City community.

4 NE 10th St., Ste. 401
southernplainsproductions.org

EXPECT THE UNEXPECTED
AT THE THEATRE CRUDE FRINGE FESTIVAL

Have you ever thought, "What if we could experience an array of live plays, much like a film festival?" If so, the Theatre Crude Fringe Festival might be just the event for you. This fall festival celebrates creativity and adventure, featuring talented performing artists nationwide. Fringe theater performances are typically one hour or less and designed to be low-tech yet highly ingenious. This style lets performers focus on their craft and showcase their skills intimately and engagingly.

Beyond the festival, there are plenty of opportunities to hone your talents. Theatre Crude offers workshops as well as the Unconventional Shorts series. There, local performers and playwrights keep it tight with original works lasting just a few minutes. Whether you're a theater enthusiast or just looking for a unique and exciting experience, the Theatre Crude Fringe Festival is worth checking out.

theatrecrude.org

42

CELEBRATE THE RITE OF SPRING
WITH THE FESTIVAL OF THE ARTS

The Festival of the Arts is a four-day community celebration of the visual and performing arts, bringing talented artists from across the nation together in Bicentennial Park. One of the festival's highlights is the opportunity to chat with the artists about their creative process and inspiration for their pieces. You'll find diverse art, from paintings and sculptures to ceramics and jewelry. The festival provides a unique opportunity to purchase unique pieces directly from the artists.

The festival is also a culinary delight. Local restaurants set up food tents throughout the park, with each one benefiting a local arts-related nonprofit, so you can indulge in your favorite treats while supporting a good cause.

For over 50 years, the Festival of the Arts has been considered a rite of spring and the Arts Council of Oklahoma City's signature event. From the beautiful art to the mouthwatering food, there's something for everyone to enjoy at this celebration of the arts.

Bicentennial Park
500 Couch Dr., 405-270-4848
artscouncilokc.com/festival-of-the-arts

PICK THE MUSIC
AT MICHAEL MURPHY'S DUELING PIANOS

Step into the vibrant world of Michael Murphy's Dueling Pianos, a haven of rock and roll transcending generations. This high-energy piano bar is situated along the Bricktown Canal and offers a unique and interactive experience for all ages, from lively 21-year-olds to spirited 90-year-olds.

Michael Murphy's was founded in 2000 and has been refined over the years to become synonymous with top-tier dueling piano entertainment. What sets Michael Murphy's apart is its interactive nature. Attendees are not just spectators; they become DJs by requesting their favorite songs through a simple form. The piano bar transforms into a request-driven extravaganza, ensuring the audience is part of the musical journey. The ambiance is further enhanced by signature drinks named after popular dueling piano songs, creating a harmonious blend of music and libations. For a seamless experience, reservations are recommended, especially for larger groups.

119 E California Ave., 405-231-5397
murphyspianobar.com

44

CATCH A MOVING PICTURE
AT RODEO CINEMA

When the first talkie movie came out in 1927, the building that now houses Rodeo Cinema refitted its equipment to be the first talkie theater in the region. Although the seats have been updated and are much comfier than they were a century ago, you can watch movies where your great-great-grandparents sat.

Operating as a nonprofit art house, Rodeo Cinema shows the films people might not be able to find elsewhere. In addition to new films, they also bring back historical movies, often with special guests who starred in them originally. Film clubs frequently meet up to discuss their favorites, and open mics and comedy shows round out the marquee to give something for everyone.

Rodeo Cinema has added a second location, too, bringing back to life the screening room in the Paramount Building on Film Row where movie house owners watched silver nitrate film to see what would bring in the customers.

2221 Exchange Ave.
701 W Sheridan Ave., Ste. 101, 405-815-3275
rodeocinema.org

ROCK OUT
AT THE DIAMOND BALLROOM

Since its opening in 1964, the Diamond Ballroom has hosted thousands of musical acts all across the board. First it was just a few Oklahoma Cityans getting together so they could have a place for Perry Jones and the Diamondaires to play. Other country stars like Conway Twitty came next, and soon the Diamond Ballroom was spreading its horizons. Musicians like Fats Domino and Jerry Lee Lewis brought in rock and roll. Powerlord added metal to the mix in 1986. Then came rockabilly, hip-hop, and just about any genre you can name.

The Diamond Ballroom is still going strong with shows as varied as death metal, folk, and electric country. If there's ever been a chance to check out the next big act when they're just starting out, or to take in an intimate concert from your favorite star on tour, it's at the Diamond Ballroom.

8001 S Eastern Ave., 405-677-9169
diamondballroom.com

CATCH MORE GREAT SHOWS AT THESE PLACES

89th Street Collective
8911 N Western Ave.
89thstreetokc.com

The Blue Door
2805 N McKinley Ave., 405-524-0738
bluedoorokc.com

The Criterion
500 E Sheridan Ave., 405-840-5500
criterionokc.com

Ice Event Center & Grille
1148 NE 36th, 405-208-4240
facebook.com/p/Ice-Event-Center-Grill-100064268186672/

The Jones Assembly
901 W Sheridan Ave., 405-212-2378
thejonesassembly.com

Resonant Head
400 SW 25th St., Ste. A
resonanthead.com

The Sanctuary
1012 N Indiana Ave.
linktr.ee/thesanctuaryok

Tower Theatre
425 NW 23rd St., 405-708-6937
towertheatreokc.com

RIVERSPORT, courtesy of Dennis Spielman

SPORTS AND RECREATION

MAKE WAVES
AT RIVERSPORT

RIVERSPORT can easily feature multiple to-do itineraries with its array of unexpected adventures, including whitewater rafting, sky bridges, zip lining, esports, surfing, and more. Despite the city standing 500 miles inland on the Great Plains, the artificial river and facilities have transformed the landscape into a world-class destination where even Olympic athletes train. However, you don't need to be an athlete to have fun at RIVERSPORT. You can conquer your fear of heights with the Rumble Drop, kayak along the Oklahoma River, and even hone your skiing skills on the indoor ski slope. From summer camps to senior dragon boating, RIVERSPORT caters to all ages, fostering an active lifestyle. Conclude your day with a meal at the Big Water Grill, savoring dishes like the Eddy Onion Cheeseburger and the Pepperoni Pizza Quesadilla.

800 Riversport Dr., 405-552-4040
riversportokc.org

KAYAK

THE STINCHCOMB WILDLIFE REFUGE

There are 170 parks in Oklahoma City, but Stinchcomb Wildlife Refuge has something unique about it: you can't walk across it! Not unless you have a set of inflatable flotation shoes.

In the early 1900s, as the city worked on water resources, it annexed part of the land to make the "Lake Overholser Sedimentation Basin" (an even more awkward name than "Stinchcomb"). Today, the waterways are better managed and the wildlife preserved while park visitors can take in the lush wetlands by boat.

There are several ways to get into Stinchcomb: park in the little lot west of Bethany High School, the lot near County Line Road, or, the best yet, paddle up from Lake Overholser. The last way might sound like the hardest, but it's actually the easiest. Park close to the water, unload your kayaks, and enjoy preserved nature just blocks from the bustling city.

NW 51st St. and N Stinchcomb Ave., 405-297-3882
okc.gov/departments/parks-recreation

TIP

Don't have your own gear? Rent from the Lake Overholser Boathouse.

CHECK OUT THE NATURAL WONDERS AT THE OKC ZOO

From humble beginnings in the 1920s, the zoo has grown in leaps through community support, including the 1949 "Children's Pennies for a New Elephant" that took in thousands of small donations to welcome Judy. In 1953, Gayle Peevey released her famous single "I Want a Hippopotamus for Christmas." Everybody in Oklahoma City wanted one, too, and soon Matilda the Hippo became a new addition.

Today, the zoo is packed with creatures big and small. Sanctuary Asia hosts an entire herd of Asian elephants; the Great EscAPE has chimpanzees, orangutans, and two troops of gorillas; and Expedition Africa brings the Serengeti to the Great Plains. While the exotic habitats are great learning experiences, the Oklahoma Trails shows locals the amazing animals we have right next door. Patrons can even have a Wild Encounter for behind-the-scenes tours and close-up feedings with some of the zoo's most incredible animals.

2000 Remington Pl., 405-424-3344
okczoo.org

49

SEEK SANCTUARY
AT MARTIN PARK NATURE CENTER

Nestled north of Lake Hefner where many residents are unaware of it, Martin Park Nature Center is a sanctuary that will make you forget about the concrete jungle surrounding it. With 2.5 miles of dirt and gravel trails that wind through scenic woodlands, the park offers a peaceful respite from the stresses of daily life. Whether walking, hiking, or jogging, you'll be surrounded by the sights and sounds of nature, from the rustling leaves of the trees to the chirping of birds. Along the way, you'll also have the opportunity to spot a wide variety of wildlife, including deer, turtles, butterflies, and more.

Martin Park Nature Center is more than just a park—it's a hub for nature exploration and education. Visitors of all ages can participate in guided hikes and educational programs. The interactive learning center provides a deeper understanding of the plants and animals that call this park home.

5000 W Memorial Rd., 405-297-1429
okc.gov/departments/parks-recreation/martin-park-nature-center

TIP

Leave your bikes, fishing poles, and pets at home as they are not permitted at Martin Park.

50

SEARCH FOR FAIRY HOUSES

AT WILL ROGERS GARDENS

A century ago, city leaders bought an old dairy farm and turned it into a "crown jewel" for the anticipated city-circling Grand Boulevard. The park has grown by leaps with the installation of the Ed Lycan Conservatory, named for OKC's first-ever parks employee; a 15-acre arboretum with many of the original trees planted by the original horticulturist, Henry Walters; and the Oklahoma City Municipal Rose Garden.

In 2020, during lockdown, the park gained popularity as a safe haven for exercise. Intriguingly, tiny painted doors started appearing on stumps and trees, evolving into a fairy village. This whimsical transformation turned out to be the brainchild of Robert Trobaugh from the OKC Parks and Recreation Department, who, seeking a hobby, created the fairy doors. Now, visitors are encouraged to explore the park and discover dozens of hidden doors, windows, and houses, making it a delightful quest for all.

3400 NW 36th St., 405-297-1394
okc.gov/recreation/will-rogers-gardens

TRAVERSE OKC'S TRAIL SYSTEM
FOR SCENIC SIGHTS

Spanning over 80 miles, Oklahoma City's network of 10 interconnected trails seamlessly weaves through the cityscape, promising recreation and fitness excitement. Whether you don your sneakers or hop on your bike, these trails lead you to virtually every corner of the city, promising an immersive journey through OKC's natural beauty and urban landscapes. Not only do the routes showcase the city's natural beauty, but scattered along, you can unveil a tapestry of public art, adding an extra layer of charm to your outdoor experience.

OKC Parks & Recreation
405-297-3882

TIP

Experience the magic of Oklahoma City under the moonlit sky with the Full Moon Bike Ride at Myriad Botanical Gardens. Designed for all levels of riders, this monthly event from April to October offers family-friendly fun and a sense of community. With a slow-paced ride not exceeding 10 miles per hour, participants have ample time to connect and enjoy the scenic beauty of downtown.

PLAY IN THE PAST
AT FLASHBACK RETRO PUB

Great Scott! Lite-Brites, liquor-packed school lockers, and both Pac-Man and Ms. Pac-Man! Step back into the 1985 of your dreams at FlashBack Retro Pub where there are dozens of arcade cabinets lined up, all set to free play: Asteroids, BurgerTime, Gyruss, Mortal Kombat, Turtles in Time, and Zaxxon, just to name a few. There are also a few diversions into later '90s and even 2000s entertainment like Mario Kart. For the truly old-school, too, there's even Skee-Ball. All this and live DJ music on Friday and Saturday nights starting after 9:30.

Playing is thirsty work, which is where FlashBack Retro Pub really delivers. As a functioning bar, it is only for ages 21 and over, giving the adults a place to play. There are hella options for signature drinks, all named after retro pop-culture faves like Care Bear, Ring Pop, Purple Rain, and Beetlejuice. FlashBack also serves 100-plus local craft beers, which are only $4 on SunDay FunDays after 5 p.m.

814 W Sheridan Ave., Ste. A, 405-633-3604
flashbackretropub.com

TIP

While FlashBack doesn't serve food, it does promote Joey's Pizza Shop just down the road. Grab a slice and bring it in!

53

CLIMB THE SILOS

Are you an adventure seeker who has no fear of heights? If so, then The Silos is the perfect place for you. What was once a grain silo has been transformed into a thrilling and unique climbing experience that you won't find anywhere else. With its towering height of 90 feet, The Silos offers a variety of climbing options including top-rope, lead, auto-belay, and bouldering. And if you're looking for something to supplement your climbing routine, the fitness nook and campus board are sure to help you get stronger.

If you're feeling especially brave, you can even climb on the outside of the building and enjoy breathtaking views of the downtown skyline. OKC's famous weather might keep you indoors, where the inside is climate-controlled, so you can climb all year round.

200 SE 4th St., 405-673-7448
stoneyardclimbing.com/the-silos

54

HAVE ALL THE FUN
AT BRICKOPOLIS

There are plenty of fun spaces in Oklahoma City, but only one offers three levels of entertainment right next to the canal: Brickopolis! The family-friendly Canal Level is a place for everyone to drop in and play arcade games. At Street Level, you can enjoy crowd-pleaser eats like pizza, wings, Tex Mex, burgers, and hot dogs. For older players, the bar has funtails, 'ritas, and plenty of frozen drinks to keep you cool. The 3rd Level is where the real excitement happens in an alien-war-zone-themed laser tag where all ages can do battle, as well as dozens more arcade games.

If those levels weren't enough, even more fun is to be had outside. Visitors can take in a round of 18 holes in miniature golf, mine for "gem" stones, or climb the walls, all while enjoying the views of the canal and waving to people on a taxi cruise.

101 S Mickey Mantle Dr., 405-516-2745
brickopolisu.com

WATCH THE CITY GO BY
ON THE WHEELER FERRIS WHEEL

The Santa Monica Pier Ferris wheel is one of the most famous amusement rides in the world. It's in the background of countless movies and television shows. Only, you won't find the original wheel in Santa Monica anymore—it's in Oklahoma City in the Wheeler District!

When Santa Monica decided to go solar with a new Ferris wheel, the classic wheel came to OKC with a $1 million refurbishment. The wheel opens each year in April and runs through November. A single ride is just $6, and visitors can get a day pass for $10, but the real bargain is to get a season pass for $20 and ride over and over again.

It's part of the Wheeler District, a riverside community built around walking and biking with access. Whether calling the Wheeler District home or just visiting, the park is a great place for picnics with the best view of downtown anywhere!

1701 S Western Ave., 405-655-8455
wheelerdistrict.com

56

SMELL THE FLOWERS
AT MYRIAD BOTANICAL GARDENS

As one of the city's most photographed destinations, the Myriad Botanical Gardens is more than a pretty place. The "Garden of Festivals" is an appropriate unofficial tagline. When they aren't doing an event that ties in with a holiday, the gardens engage with the community through educational tours and classes, diversifying Oklahoma's green canopy. You can enjoy outdoor movies during summer, ride under the moonlight during the Full Moon Bike Ride, or learn to dance during Dancing in the Gardens. One of their largest events, Pumpkinville, takes place in October and features imaginative displays of over 30,000 pumpkins.

You can visit the Crystal Bridge Conservatory any time of the year. It includes 13,000 square feet of plant display area in two distinct climates: the Tropical Wet Zone and the Tropical Dry Zone at the north end. Before leaving, make sure to stop by the gift shop.

301 W Reno Ave., 405-445-7080
myriadgardens.org

TIP

If you become a member, you can enjoy free admission to the Crystal Bridge, free entry to select events, and discounts.

EXPLORE SCISSORTAIL PARK

With so many activities to choose from all in one place, you'll be able to explore the playground, fly a kite, walk a trail, skate in the rink, paddle in the pond, play sports, have a picnic, and so much more. Whether you're looking for a place to relax and unwind or a place to get your heart pumping, Scissortail Park has everything you need to have a great time. If you find yourself hungry, stop at SPARK for burgers, bites, and cold delights. You'll also often find food trucks along the east side of the park.

Be sure to come to the seasonal outdoor farmers market on Saturdays from April to October. This producer-only market only allows homegrown, handmade, or vendor-created productions from locally owned operations within Oklahoma.

300 SW 7th St., 405-445-6277
scissortailpark.org

FLOAT THE CANAL
WITH BRICKTOWN WATER TAXI

Since the first boat cast off in 1999 down the Bricktown Canal, over two million passengers have ridden the fleet of boats, getting a unique view of what urban renewal can do as old warehouses have become restaurants, corporate offices, and entertainment venues. The southern end of the journey sails through the Oklahoma City Land Run Monument, a string of larger-than-life statues.

The 40-minute regular tour is a must, but that's only the beginning. For history buffs, the Bricktown History Tour shares tales of early Oklahoma City. ArtAFloatOKC brings even more ways to enjoy the canal with light shows, horticultural displays, and music. The Showboat Concert Series brings a variety of genres from local musicians to entertain. Haunted History Cruises in the fall tell spooky stories from Oklahoma City's past. For holiday fun, Caroling Cruises invite passengers to sing along as they sail by the Christmas lights of Bricktown.

111 S Mickey Mantle Dr., 405-234-8294
bricktownwatertaxi.com

SCREAM FOR THE THRILLS
OF FRONTIER CITY

From the adrenaline-pumping thrills of soaring to the highest heights to the gripping spectacles of gunfighters engaging in epic old-west-style duels, Frontier City blends the allure of the Wild West with the excitement of a world-class amusement park (but minus the robot drama of *Westworld*). The multifaceted destination also has kid-friendly rides, multiple dining options, and water rides like the iconic Mystery River Log Flume, guaranteed to get you soaked. Be sure to check out the famed stunt and musical shows in the Crack Axel Canyon amphitheater.

As the seasons change, so does the character of Frontier City. When Halloween approaches, the park undergoes a sinister transformation, unveiling its much-anticipated Fright Fest. During this spine-chilling season, families can indulge in daytime thrills that cater to all ages, while, as night descends, the bravest souls can brace themselves for the scariest frights that haunt the shadows.

11501 N I-35 Service Rd., 405-478-2140
sixflags.com/frontiercity

TIP

Plan to begin your day at attractions farthest from the main gate. Not only will you beat the crowds racing to the closest attractions, but you'll be right next to the exit as you wrap up your visit!

SEE IF YOU CAN
ESCAPE OKC'S ESCAPE ROOMS

For thrill-seekers needing a clever challenge to beat, an escape room is the place to go. Whether in small groups or individuals teamed with strangers, players search for clues around a locked room to determine how to get out. This problem-solving works as a perfect team-building exercise with players needing to cooperate and think creatively to solve the puzzle within the allotted time. There's no life or death involved, just your own wits.

Oklahoma City has several options to choose from, each with its own flair and flurry of original escape rooms. The Sanctuary Escape Games features Hollywood-level style set designs with multi-room levels of puzzles to escape. The Lost Dutchman's Mine will make you feel like Indian Jones as you try to escape the lost mine.

7650 W Reno Ave., 405-726-1022
thesanctuaryokc.com/escape

OTHER ESCAPE ROOMS TO TRY

Baker Street Escapes
1004 N Hudson Ave., Ste. 104
405-837-8481
bakerstreetescapes.com

Breakout Games
2501 W Memorial Rd., Ste. 227
405-731-9192
breakoutgames.com/oklahoma-city

The Escape OKC
912 NW 23rd St.
405-898-8999
theescapeokc.com

TAKE YOUR PUP
TO SOLO'S PARK & PUB

People love hanging out at pubs, and people love dogs, so why not hang out at the pub with your dog (and everyone else's)? Solo's Park & Pub brings together the best while always being careful to ensure everyone has a good time. Pups need to be updated on all their vaccines and play by the rules so that they can enjoy an on-leash patio and an off-leash dog park. The people, meanwhile, can enjoy a restaurant and bar by themselves or head out to play with the pups.

Solo's calendar is packed with weekly events and special occasions. Drop in on Tuesday for trivia and tacos, Wednesdays for musical bingo, Thursdays for free-to-play bingo, and much more on Fridays and the weekends! Whether your idea of a good time is playing poker or spelling bees, Solo's has you covered.

13310 Pawnee Dr., 405-849-5990
solosparkandpub.com

HIDE AND GO BIKE
ON THURSDAYS

The Hide and Go Bike (HGB) event is a weekly gathering in the warm months that celebrates inclusivity, fun, and community for cyclists. HGB Thursdays provide a welcoming environment where all types of bikes and riders are embraced with open arms. The event is free, emphasizing the idea that participants need only bring themselves and their bikes to join the 10-to-12-mile ride at a leisurely pace of 10 miles per hour. Participants get to discover new parts of the city during the two-to-two-and-a-half-hour ride, with stops incorporated along the way. The event not only promotes a healthy and active lifestyle but also serves as a means to familiarize people with different neighborhoods, breaking down barriers and encouraging a sense of connection to the larger community.

Meet up at Mesta Park, 1900 N Shartel Ave.
Instagram: @hideandgobike

63

FOLLOW EXOTIC RACING
AT REMINGTON PARK

Remington Park is exciting year-round with quarter horse racing from the spring into early summer, thoroughbred horse racing all through the fall, and the Coffee and Cars the first Saturday morning of every month with classic cars and custom jobs for all gearheads. However, there is one annual event that packs surprises for even the most seasoned horse-track veteran: exotic animal racing.

It's a charity event that will leave people wondering what could be next. Every year is different, depending on what animals and riders are available. Many of the races are with creatures not too different from horses, such as miniature donkeys or zebras, as well as enormous Clydesdales standing over six feet tall. Other critters are something else entirely, such as specially trained racing ostriches that can carry riders as fast as 25 miles per hour down the track.

1 Remington Pl., 405-424-1000
remingtonpark.com

GO GLAMPING
AT ORR FAMILY FARM

Dr. Glen Orr and his family opened their farm to visitors in 2004 as a family-friendly destination where kids and grown-ups alike could learn more about agriculture and play fun games. It's famous for its petting zoo and pumpkin patch, but those are just the beginning. Today the farm offers a fishing pond, a giant jumping pillow, a cannon blaster shooting gallery, and even human foosball. It's so much fun, it's hard to leave for the night. And now you don't have to!

Overnight guests can stay in cabins in the forms of larger-than-life Conestoga wagons and teepees. They won't be roughing it: this is glamping, not just camping. Facilities include a swim spa, campfire, fridge, microwave, and even snack machines. Glampers also receive year-round access to many of the activities usually closed for winter, such as bottle-feeding baby animals.

14400 S Western Ave., 405-799-3276
orrfamilyfarm.com

GLEAM THE CUBE
AT MAT HOFFMAN ACTION SPORTS PARK

Just south of downtown rests the biggest and most daring skate park in the state, one of *National Geographic*'s top 10 in the country. Named for X Games gold medalist Mat Hoffman, the action park stretches over 26,000 square feet, suitable for anyone with the right nerves and a set of wheels, whether BMX, skateboards, or Rollerblades. While light on the easy stuff for beginners, the park is packed with challenges for even the biggest pros. There's the bowl course with a three-shape panda bowl, a 10-foot over-vert, and an 11-foot half-pipe. Then there's the street course with handrails, stairs, and ledges for skaters who want a flavor of real-life antics without hassling anyone.

It's fittingly part of Manuel Perez Park, named for the Congressional-Medal-of-Honor-winning World War II paratrooper. Thrill-seekers today are trying to catch some air rather than leaping out of it, but the excitement is still all there.

1700 S Robinson Ave., 405-297-2211
visitokc.com/listing/mat-hoffman-action-sports-park/868

66

RACE
IN THE MEMORIAL MARATHON

Every April, Oklahoma City commemorates the 168 lives lost in the 1995 attack that rocked downtown. What began as a fundraiser for the memorial and museum has become one of the most famous races in the country and an official Boston-qualifying race. Today tens of thousands of people race with all proceeds still going to the memorial and museum as we "Run to Remember."

Rather than being a single racing event, the Memorial Marathon is actually a string of events as part of the Why We Run Weekend Series. Racers may compete in the 26.2-mile full marathon, or they may try the half-marathon, or they can be a part of the 5K. There is even the Kids Marathon where kids have plenty of time to log their miles ahead with just the last 1.2 miles being in person, showing that remembering isn't just a one-time thing but something we work toward every day.

okcmarathon.com

BLOW GLASS
WITH BLUE SAGE STUDIOS

Discover the art of glassblowing at Blue Sage Studios, where creativity meets craftsmanship. You can create your own one-of-a-kind glass piece under the guidance of skilled artisans. Choose from various options such as ornaments, flowers, or paperweights, each taking approximately 10 to 15 minutes to complete. Select from a palette of vibrant colors to personalize your creation. The intricate process involves shaping molten glass, rolling it in color, and using specialized techniques to craft your chosen design. The studio provides all the necessary supplies, and you can keep your masterpieces.

Keep in mind you can only take home your glass art pieces after they undergo a 12-hour annealing process, which ensures their durability. Wear comfortable cotton clothing and closed-toe shoes for the hot studio environment, and enjoy the experience with provided safety glasses. Whether you're a budding glass artist or a curious observer, Blue Sage Studios invites you to witness the mesmerizing art of glassblowing firsthand.

1218-C N Western Ave., 405-601-2583
bluesagestudios.com

First Americans Museum, courtesy of Dennis Spielman

CULTURE AND HISTORY

68

TOUCH THE ART
AT FACTORY OBSCURA

Factory Obscura's Mix-Tape is not just an art installation; it's a permanent creative journey inspired by the art of making and giving mixtapes as gifts. Unlike traditional art exhibits, Factory Obscura encourages visitors to touch, interact, and explore, breaking away from the conventional boundaries of art engagement. Factory Obscura is committed to inclusivity—their experiences are designed for everyone, regardless of age, and they prioritize accessibility, ensuring wheelchair access with alternate routes for areas that require climbing.

As Factory Obscura established Mix-Tape as their first permanent exhibit, you can expect an ever-evolving-and-changing environment. The venue promises a unique visual experience and hosts events and parties, turning each visit into a celebration. With annual passes available, providing unlimited admission and exclusive perks, Factory Obscura invites everyone to be part of this artistic journey, creating a space where art becomes a timeless and inclusive adventure.

25 NW 9th St., 405-367-1578
factoryobscura.com

TIP

Try pushing different combinations of buttons on the Boom Box out front for a whimsical surprise.

GET INSPIRED
AT OKLAHOMA CONTEMPORARY

In 2020, the new Oklahoma Contemporary complex opened on Broadway to highlight the awesome art created not just by those in the past but by the diverse artists living today. The 8,000 square feet of galleries give visitors plenty of room to check out the amazing works artists are producing in the moment, and the exhibits frequently change out to show off even more talent. The Campbell Art Park shows additional art outside, and the Te Ata Theater gives space for screenings and live shows.

The greatest lesson learned at the Contemporary, however, is that anyone can be an artist. Camp Contemporary offers classes for kids during spring and summer breaks, giving them experience with color, sewing, and even clay birdhouses. Studio School gives everyone the chance to learn more about fiber arts, ceramics, digital media, and more. Schedules are flexible with classes lasting four or eight weeks and one-day workshops that focus on a single project. Everyone has an artist in them ready to step out and shine.

11 NW 11th St., 405-951-0000
oklahomacontemporary.org

STROLL
THE ASIAN NIGHT MARKET

Oklahoma City boasts one of the largest Vietnamese communities in the United States, which has revitalized the northern end of Classen into a vibrant neighborhood packed with businesses of all kinds including bakeries and some of the best pho restaurants anywhere. Lunar New Year is of course a major celebration early each year, but there is no place like the Asian District Night Market in the fall to hear the music, taste the foods, and see the wares and crafts of the vendors.

The Night Market closes down a few blocks of Classen to set up tents and line up food trucks to feed the crowd. It's the perfect time to try something new like Laotian coffee or shaking beef salad. In nearby Military Park, where the statue stands of American and Vietnamese soldiers side by side, the stage is kept busy with ceremonial dances as well as fresh new music from Oklahoma creatives.

2520 N Classen Blvd.
asiandistrictok.com/anmf

71

DISCOVER OUR STATE'S ROOTS
AT THE FIRST AMERICANS MUSEUM

The state and city's name comes from two Choctaw words, "Okla" and "Homma," meaning "Red People," a continuous reminder of how important native culture is to our world. The First Americans Museum is the perfect place to learn about the 39 nations recognized living here today. Exhibitions showcase the history and legend of the First Americans and display today's great representations and unfortunate misrepresentations. Learn history firsthand with interactive features like the 270-degree Origins Theater, a powwow van, and virtual chunkey or "hand game" for a bit of esports.

The museum also hosts fantastic eating. Thirty Nine Restaurant focuses its menu on maintaining and reimagining traditional dishes based on ingredients still grown and harvested around Oklahoma as First Americans have done for generations. The Arbor Cafe also offers native-inspired food along with specialty coffees and teas unlike anywhere else you can find.

659 First Americans Blvd., 405-594-2100
famok.org

TIP

Keep an eye on the FAM's event calendar for awesome times like the pop culture fair IndigiPopX, the New Year's Stickball Game, and the Potato Dance World Championship.

TAKE IN THE BEAUTY
OF THE OKC MUSEUM OF ART

Stretching up 55 feet at the entrance of the Donald W. Reynolds Visual Arts Center, 2,400 pieces of handblown Dale Chihuly glass form one of OKC's greatest icons. Its official name is the Eleanor Blake Kirkpatrick Memorial Tower, and it is only the beginning to the city's Museum of Art.

The permanent collection at the MOA holds much more of Chihuly's work, along with creations by Georgia O'Keeffe, Alexander Calder, Thomas Moran, and many more. With frequent new exhibitions coming through, Oklahoma Cityans can see world-class art pieces right at home as they tour the nation. The museum is free for kids 17 and younger, making it a perfect family outing.

While you're taking in the museum, make some art of your own! The museum hosts various classes as well as Drop-In Art activities every third Saturday from 11 a.m. to 4 p.m.

415 Couch Dr., 405-236-3100
okcmoa.com

TIP

Visit the Noble Theater for lectures, live performances, and special film screenings of documentaries, remastered movies, and countdowns to the Oscars showing nominees' work.

73

HAVE A "COO" TIME
AT THE PIGEON MUSEUM

It might be hard to believe that there's a whole museum dedicated to pigeons, but, once you visit it, your perspective on pigeons will never be the same! Pigeons have been alongside humans for thousands of years as one of the first domesticated animals. They've been a food source, pets, and even war heroes. Brave pigeon couriers carried messages over battlefields for centuries up to the World Wars. Because speed is so important to delivery, pigeon racing grew into a sport that today has thousands compete in fascinating time trials.

The American Pigeon Museum & Library also provides plenty of information about fancy pigeons, the many breeds that have been bred to look beautiful. There are fantail pigeons looking like tiny peacocks, fluffy Jacobin pigeons, huge king pigeons, colorful archangel pigeons, and so many more to check out. With free admission, the price can't be beat!

2300 NE 63rd St., 405-478-5155
theamericanpigeonmuseum.org

TIP

Come to the Pigeon Museum on a nice, warm day, and you can find many of the fancy pigeons who live there getting some sun. You might even be able to pet them, but don't get your hopes up on borrowing one to send secret messages.

TRAVEL BACK IN TIME
AT THE NATIONAL COWBOY & WESTERN HERITAGE MUSEUM

There couldn't be a more fitting place for the National Cowboy & Western Heritage Museum than Oklahoma City. It began as a cowboy museum in 1955, but soon people recognized there is so much more to the historical picture of the West. Today the museum houses more than 28,000 pieces of Western and Native American artwork and artifacts telling the ongoing story of the West.

Galleries in the museum organize the materials into interactive exhibits packed with eye-opening information. Visitors learn about cowboys, rodeos, and the grand tradition of western films. They also take in the huge collection of art depicting the diverse range of people who helped make the West what it is today. While you're there, amble through Prosperity Junction, a replica turn-of-the-20th-century cattle town where you can see yourself working the herd as cowhands still do today.

1700 NE 63rd St., 405-478-2250
nationalcowboymuseum.org

TIP

Take a stroll through the gardens behind the museum, which are also the last resting places for some of rodeo's most famous animals like Tornado and Five Minutes to Midnight.

75

WALK THE ART GALLERIES IN THE PASEO ARTS DISTRICT

Built in 1929 as a shopping district, the Paseo Arts District has maintained its Spanish Revival architecture throughout the years. The original stucco buildings and clay tile roofs are still intact. Nowadays, the Paseo houses over 20 galleries and more than 80 artists, all of which are within walking distance. The galleries are interspersed with incredible restaurants, shoe and clothing boutiques, gift shops, and performance venues. Grab yourself a vegan doughnut from Holey Rollers or a slice of pizza from Sauced if you want something portable to eat while you explore.

On every first Friday of the month, rain or shine, from 6 p.m. to 9 p.m., the Paseo hosts the First Friday Gallery Walk. During this event, visitors can explore new work from studio owners and guest artists, enjoy live music, and experience a unique, family-friendly atmosphere.

3024 Paseo, 405-525-2688
thepaseo.org

TIP

The Paseo Arts Festival takes place every Memorial Day weekend. The festival attracts over 60,000 visitors annually and showcases the works of over 90 juried artists nationwide.

76

EXPERIMENT
AT SCIENCE MUSEUM OKLAHOMA

Science Museum Oklahoma immerses visitors in a world of wonder and discovery as soon as they walk inside. You can explore the stars in their planetarium, tinker with engineering projects in the Tinkering Garage, or watch science demonstrations that bring science to life. The museum is committed to making science accessible and enjoyable for everyone, with quiet spaces if things get too loud. Plus, with their rotating exhibitions, you can visit multiple times and have a new experience each time.

Boasting over 390,000 square feet of interactive science exhibits, art, and history, Science Museum Oklahoma has something to offer everyone. Their mission is to inspire curiosity and promote learning, and they accomplish this goal brilliantly.

2020 Remington Pl., 405-602-6664
sciencemuseumok.org

TIP

Leave the kids at home with SMO21. This adults-only night at the museum lets you experience the museum entirely differently, with cocktails, music, and experiments that are too advanced for the younger ones.

BE WOWED

AT DEADCENTER FILM FESTIVAL

The film scene in Oklahoma is blowing up, and much of it is thanks to deadCenter, which *MovieMaker* magazine counted among the "Top 20 Coolest Film Festivals in the World." Every summer, filmmakers from around the world gather to show off their stuff right here in the middle of America. It's the chance to see "exciting new short films, insightful documentaries, hilarious comedies, scary monster movies and the best independent films" as well as a movie star or two coming to town. Screenings take place in multiple locations around downtown since just one spot can't hold them all!

Beyond the summer festival, deadCenter keeps busy year-round. Its Continuum program highlights diverse communities around the state with inclusive films. Meanwhile, the school-based Education Tour encourages creativity, teamwork, and confidence among Oklahoma students as they make three-minute movies.

223 S Walker Ave., 405-246-9233
deadcenterfilm.org

TIP

Know a young filmmaker? Check out deadCenter's Teen Board and its call for films created by high school students.

COME TOGETHER
AT JUNETEENTH ON THE EAST

Juneteenth on the East stands as a symbol of unity, freedom, and community on the Eastside of Oklahoma City. This annual celebration, rich in history and culture, has evolved into a timeless event that brings people together to rejoice in the spirit of emancipation. At the heart of Juneteenth on the East is the With Love Project, a brainchild of activist-artist JABEE and the Oklahoma Mural Syndicate in 2020. Today, the With Love Project has grown into a separate nonprofit organization dedicated to bringing public art, cultural events, and education to the Eastside of Oklahoma City. A monthlong celebration filled with diverse activities, such as brunch crawls, 5K runs, and panel discussions, culminates in a grand festival. Come together in the spirit of Juneteenth to honor the past, celebrate the present, and pave the way for a future where unity and freedom reign supreme.

withloveokc.org/juneteenth

CELEBRATE DIVERSITY
WITH PRIDE MONTH

Celebrate love, diversity, and acceptance during Pride Month in Oklahoma City, where a vibrant array of events fills the calendar with excitement, artistry, and celebration. Among the highlights are PrideFest and Pride on 39th, two signature events that showcase the city's commitment to inclusivity.

PrideFest, held at the picturesque Scissortail Park, has swiftly become a cornerstone event for the LGBTQIA2S+ community in OKC. With an impressive lineup of local and international entertainers, PrideFest provides a dynamic platform for connection and visibility, reinforcing OKC's reputation as an open and welcoming city.

For a historical touch, Pride on 39th Street, a major Pride fixture since 1988, has evolved into OKC Pride Inc., a nonprofit organization. This group orchestrates OKC's annual Pride week, transforming it into the largest privately held event in Oklahoma. Tens of thousands from the state and surrounding areas gather, turning 39th Street into a regional Pride destination.

okpridealliance.org
prideon39th.com

80

SEE THE LATEST CREATIONS AT THE OKLAHOMA STATE FAIR

Every September as the summer heat begins to draw back, we gather up our best produce, most creative projects, and anything altogether new to share with one another. In fact, we've been having state fairs even before statehood in 1907!

Agriculture stands as one of the most important parts of the fair with 4-H and FFA exhibits. The Dairy Discovery Zone shows how dairy farmers take care of their herds while feeding the state, and the Barnyard Birthing Center allows veterinarians to show the miracle of life.

Education is wonderful, but that's only the start to the fair. People come from across the region for exciting entertainment and carnival rides. Most famous, of course, is the food. From deep-fried Oreos to freeze-dried Jolly Rancher cotton candy, the fair is a chance to experience something you've truly never tried before.

3001 General Pershing Blvd., 405-948-6700
okstatefair.com

MEET SIR INDIANA BONES AT THE MUSEUM OF OSTEOLOGY

With more than 800 specimens in over 40 exhibits in a two-level museum stretching over 7,000 square feet, there is nowhere quite like Skeletons: Museum of Osteology. Guests can see the fascinating interworking of bones from tiny mice all the way up to whales hanging from the ceiling. The Explorer's Corner gives guests the chance to test their knowledge and handle actual bones of Oklahoma creatures, showing how to tell the difference between a beaver and a possum.

On top of its educational merit and its outright coolness featuring so many skeletons, the Museum of Osteology took the internet by storm with its "museum cat," Sir Indiana Bones. It's a sensible idea to have an office cat patrolling a facility near so many fields where mice might wander in. Today the kitty not only takes pics with fans but also raises funds for animal welfare with iconic merch.

10301 S Sunnylane Rd., 405-814-0006
skeletonmuseum.com

DRIVE

OKC'S ROUTE 66

Want to go on one of the greatest American road trips without ever leaving town? Then you need to get your kicks on OKC's stretch of Route 66!

The Mother Road runs from Chicago to Los Angeles over some 2,248 miles. Where exactly it crossed through Oklahoma City depends on which year it was during the long reign of Route 66 as "America's Main Street." It's been realigned and updated through the years, meaning you could come down I-35 between Witcher and the zoo for today's technical stretch of highway or cruise Kelley Avenue from Memorial Road on down to the Capitol on Lincoln for a more historical view.

Some iconic sites include the Milk Bottle Building, the Gold Dome, Route 66 Bowl, and Owl Court Suites. The truss bridge over Lake Overholser has been in the backgrounds of numerous road trip movies and TV shows.

okc.gov/visitors/route-66-in-okc

TIP

Another name for Route 66 is the Will Rogers Highway, commemorating "Oklahoma's native son."

83

SEE WHAT'S NEW
ON THE PLAZA WALLS

Oklahoma has seen a burst of murals, and there's no place better in the state to check out truly modern art than in the Plaza District. The Oklahoma Mural Syndicate has been painting—and repainting—the long alleyways behind the Plaza since 2015. Space running 12 feet tall and some 400 feet long gives plenty of room for local and regional artists to get creative. It's divided into 30 to 40 sections, giving literally dozens of canvases for enormous art in nearly every style imaginable. It could be brightly colored geometric shapes, grotesques, cartoons, vivid realism, cubism, surrealism, and on and on. Whatever it is, it's always vibrant.

In a few months, the space is cleared out and done up all over again with new work by more artists, keeping the Plaza Walls a destination to return to again and again.

1745 NW 16th St., Ste. F4, 405-252-0569
plazawalls.org

TIP

Come to the Plaza District Festival in the summer for the Plaza Walls Mural Expo to witness the artists in action.

STAND ON THE SHOULDERS OF GIANTS

AT THE OKLAHOMA HALL OF FAME

What do OU's first president David Ross Boyd, baseball star Johnny Bench, guitarist Charlie Christian, and ballerina Maria Tallchief Paschen all have in common? They're all in the Oklahoma Hall of Fame!

In 1927, Anna B. Korn thought that our then-20-year-old state should commemorate the folks who made Oklahoma great with a hall of fame. Since then, the list has grown to more than 700 including philanthropists, civic leaders, educators, and celebrities. The wide range of inductees shows just how many hands it takes to build a state and inspires everyone who visits to make their own mark. You might even be an inductee yourself one day!

The Oklahoma Hall of Fame at the Gaylord-Pickens Museum has rotating exhibits telling the stories of the many hall-of-famers as well as permanent galleries with plenty of activities for learners of all ages.

1400 Classen Dr., 405-235-4458
oklahomahof.com

PICK SOME STRINGS
AT THE AMERICAN BANJO MUSEUM

Walking down the sidewalk of Sheridan east of the railroad tracks, you'll start hearing banjo music twanging. It invites you into the beautiful brick building that houses an entire world of music. The first exhibit covers four centuries in eight minutes, showing how African instruments evolved into the banjo through the South. Banjos hit their heyday in the early 20th century with performers in demand by crowds of thousands and among the first music broadcast on radio. Relics of the past include racks of gold-plated banjos, showing just how important this instrument has been to American culture.

Visitors aren't only going to see the past: they're going to play in the present and future, too! Exhibits show popular musicians of today still making use of the banjo, and the upstairs includes a replica of a Your Father's Mustache club where banjo performances continue with lunchtime concerts and nighttime jam sessions.

9 E Sheridan Ave., 405-604-2793
americanbanjomuseum.com

TIP

Newcomers to the banjo can come to monthly Pick-a-Tune group lessons, hosted by OKC's own Lucas Ross, who was inspired by comedian Steve Martin (whose Mark Twain Prize banjo awarded by the Kennedy Center rests in the museum).

Paseo District, courtesy of Jeff Provine

SHOPPING AND FASHION

STOP
ALONG AUTOMOBILE ALLEY

When the state was only three years old, entrepreneurs saw potential, bringing car dealers to a strip of North Broadway. These were different times when many cars came custom ordered and models were kept in upstairs garages. While most cities ended up tearing down their automobile alleys, OKC's neon lights are lit, shining up and down the street like yesteryear.

Of course, people don't come to Automobile Alley to shop for cars these days. Today the district is home to restaurants, boutique shops, and businesses as a vibrant part of the cityscape. Most of the buildings are converted from their originals while keeping the uniqueness of reclaimed urbanization. Check out some of the best food and drink in OKC at places like Broadway 10, Katiebug's Sips & Sweets, and Vanessa House Beer Company. As for shopping, you have to check local favorites like Common Dear, Plenty Mercantile, Shop Good, and more.

405-235-3500
automobilealley.org

TIP

Automobile Alley is famed for its lights all year long, but there's nothing like the holiday lights every year at Christmas. Check out the Lights on Broadway display as part of OKC's Downtown in December.

87

DISCOVER WHAT YOU NEVER KNEW YOU NEEDED
AT BLUE SEVEN

Whether you're from Oklahoma City or just passing through, there's just about no better shop for that Big Friendly spirit than Blue Seven. A proud promoter of everything Oklahoma, Blue Seven connects with its customers in the same way it connects with its artists and designers, bringing everyone together for a stronger community. It's the perfect place to get branded clothing, hats, prints, and collectibles showing Oklahoma art, country chic themes, Route 66, or just about anything that hollers "OKC!"

In addition to its top-notch clothing collection, Blue Seven stocks games, stuffies, and kitchen gadgets. Make your kitchen livelier with Buddy the dog-shaped spoon holder or a lunch box disguised as a guitar case. There's no question why Blue Seven routinely makes the list for best shopping experience and the go-to stop for the giftee who has everything.

7518 N May Ave., 405-604-5199
myblueseven.com

88

POP DOWN
TO MIDTOWN

With its famous sign over the plaza court building, Midtown has been a go-to destination since the days of the first streetcar in OKC. The neighborhood is packed with boutique shops, tantalizing restaurants, and fun times with escape rooms and Dust Bowl Lanes. Shopping favorites include the Black Scintilla, Chirps & Cheers, NASH Engineered Fashion, Nhu Avenue, and more. Watch the calendar for Midtown Walkabout events with specials and activities as well as the Midtown Cool Down.

While Midtown is a good time all year round, it especially shines every spring and winter with the Independent Shopkeepers Association's pop-up shops. Geodesic domes pop up to turn a grassy lot into a busy mall. Most famous are the Holiday Pop-Up Shops in December for the perfect present, but the spring Pop-Up Market can't be beat with its wide variety of local vendors offering vintage finds, handmade crafts, and artistic innovations.

405-235-3500
midtownokc.com
okcpopups.com

PEEK IN THE WINDOWS
AT THE PLAZA DISTRICT

This famed shopping neighborhood rose up around the original trolley line turnaround in 1926, and today people still enjoy the broad sidewalks with plenty to see (and eat)! Grab a slice at Empire and take in the Plaza Walls murals—but the best time spent at the Plaza is checking out the many unique shops. Bad Granny's Bazaar is packed with vintage clothes, books, furniture, and just about everything you could want. Want something on the weirder side? Dig through Dig It OKC for some of the coolest alternative gear. The Refillery by Local Lather gives shoppers a chance to buy local, homemade, small-batch products in bulk while they refill containers, cutting down on landfill waste. DNA Galleries hosts local artists for the freshest in Oklahoma creations. Just to name a few!

1745 NW 16th St.
plazadistrict.org

TIP

Come out on the second Friday of the month for LIVE! on the Plaza for live music and extra vendors. Some months even have special themes, such as the famous GHOULS! on the Plaza in October.

FLIP THROUGH THE PAGES

AT FULL CIRCLE BOOKSTORE

Imagine a bookstore with its oak shelves packed with 60,000 titles and lined by rolling ladders. There are cozy chairs next to the toasty fireplace, and live jazz trickles from the café at the end of the shop. Sound idyllic? Then experience it for real at Full Circle Bookstore!

Climb on the ladders to reach your next great find, but don't try to slide like Belle singing; that's a safety issue. As the largest independent, locally owned bookstore in the state, you never know what you'll come across while you peruse the shelves.

Once you have your new book (or stack of new books!), stick around for Full Circle's famed events with authors reading and signing, musical performances, and special get-togethers for crafts, lectures, and literary trivia.

1900 Northwest Expy., 405-842-2900
fullcirclebooks.com

OTHER GREAT BOOKSHOPS IN OKC

Commonplace Books
1325 N Walker Ave., Ste. 138, 405-534-4540
commonplacebooksokc.com

Belle Books Boutique & More
1742 NE 23rd St., Ste. B, 405-506-5074

The Floating Bookshop
617 W Sheridan Ave.

Literati Press Bookshop
3022 Paseo, 405-882-7032
literatipressok.com

Nappy Roots Books
3621 N Lottie Ave., 405-896-0203

Second Story Books
718 Culbertson Dr., 405-673-7160
secondstorybooksokc.com

91

REUSE
AT DEAD PEOPLE'S STUFF

One of the best reasons to visit antique stores and new-to-you shops is to keep genuine treasures from disappearing to a landfill. Dead People's Stuff takes that tradition to the highest level, pulling the literal doors off hinges of buildings that are coming down. This allows buyers a handmade door with unique fixtures that they might otherwise have never seen—or would have had to spend a ton to buy new! Instead, with a little elbow grease, you can have a door that impresses guests before they even step into your house.

It's not just doors in Dead People's Stuff's 40,000-square-foot warehouse. The building is filled with one-of-a-kind finds including chandeliers, door knockers, leaded glass windows, mantels, and endless decor. Step inside to find antique metal signs advertising businesses of yesteryear, Philco radios, even swinging butter churns. Someone once loved it, and now it's your turn.

1900 Linwood Blvd., 405-232-0759
deadpeoplesstuffok.com

WATCH A LONGHORN PARADE
IN STOCKYARDS CITY

Everyone loves a parade, and there's none quite like watching cowboys drive a whole herd of longhorns down the street amid a cheering crowd. Stockyards Stampede brings the classic days of the range to modern folks with a genuine chuck wagon camp, petting zoo, and world-class steak cook-off. It's important to remember where our food comes from and the hard work it takes to keep hungry bellies fed.

All year round, Stockyards City is the center of Oklahoma's cow country. It's still one of the largest cattle auctions in the world, and the whole district thrives around genuine Western life. Shops offer handcrafted hats and boots. Cattlemen's Steakhouse has been the place to get a steak for over a century, and Stockyards Sarsaparilla offers a wide range of sweet treats for dessert. The Horseshoe Museum displays the fascinating life of a farrier and the development of modern shoeing. Boxcar Woody makes the old new again, literally, with reclaimed wood from boxcars fashioned into stylish rustic furniture.

2401 Exchange Ave., Ste. D, 405-235-7267
stockyardscity.org

FIND FOOD, FUN, AND FASHION
AT CLASSEN CURVE

Location, location, location, they say, and the junction of Classen, Grand, Western, and Northwest 63rd, only a step away from I-44, has it all. Classen Curve, the Triangle at Classen Curve, and Nichols Hills Plaza have grown into a premier modern corner for all your food, fun, and fashion needs. It offers plenty of dining options including locations of Oklahoma City classics like Empire Slice, Tucker's Onion Burgers, and Roxy's Ice Cream Social. For a special treat, hit up *Cupcake Wars* winner Green Goodies for some of the best baking in the nation!

Classen Curve is more than just food. They have shops for apparel, home, health—just about anything you could need. There are choices for every kind of fitness gym, perfect for your preference in exercise. Or, just come to hang out with the family in the Yard to play outdoor games and have a picnic.

6100 N Western Ave., 405-902-2505
classencurve.com

TIP

Check out the calendar for fun events like the Redbud Classic, Boo Bash, and CK and Company's Fashion for a Passion. Every Thursday, Red Coyote's Pack Pint Run invites all abilities to come out for a fun race and a drink together.

GET FRESH
AT FARMERS PUBLIC MARKET

A century ago, farmers in the countryside around Oklahoma City needed a place to get their produce directly to customers. The tradition still lives on today at the Farmers Public Market with regular farmers markets every Saturday from 9 a.m. to 2 p.m. People can't live on food alone, so the upstairs hosts concerts, fairs, and weddings just as they did when Bob Wills and Hank Williams Sr. were playing there.

The 40,000-square-foot main building is only the start. Behind it, there are vintage shops and antique stalls covering 20,000 square feet in the mall. Once you've checked out the whole thing, you've truly seen them all!

Delmar Gardens Food Truck Park is also at the market, giving people plenty of opportunities for a quick bite while they shop or take in a show. With enough stalls for 10 trucks at a time, it's routinely voted one of OKC's top food truck parks.

311 S Klein Ave., 405-232-6506
okcfarmersmarket.com

BE CURIOUS
AT CRAIG'S EMPORIUM

Looking for something out of the ordinary? Craig's has you covered. Nicknamed "The Most Magical Place in Oklahoma," the store is packed with mystic stones and crystals, talismans, oils and herbs for smudge, tarot cards, and plenty more supernatural wonders. Yet that isn't all: a lot of the items in Craig's are simply a lot of fun, like *Ghostbusters* memorabilia or gag greeting cards.

Arriving at Craig's is an immediate feast for the senses. The air is filled with the smell of incense and the trickling of the indoor waterfall. Every corner has its own theme, whether dedicated to LGBTQIA2S+ gifts, Egyptology, knights and armor, or home decor fitting for Halloween all year round. Their esoteric library cannot be beaten with a vast collection on nearly every mystic topic as well as recreation, history, and self-help. You'll find something you never knew existed but now wouldn't want to live without.

1209 NW 23rd St., 405-524-9447
craigsemporium.com

96

GRAB ALL THE JERKY YOU COULD WANT

AT JERKY.COM

It started with five flavors in 2008, and the selection at Jerky.com has now grown into more than 100 flavors including pale ale beer, scorpion pepper, tequila lime, au jus, and just about anything anyone can come up with. While it may seem like a far-off digital warehouse, it's actually a proud Oklahoma City institution with its store right in Bricktown. Drop by to try not only a huge variety of flavors for beef jerky but also jerky made from chicken, venison, elk, wild boar, alligator, and even kangaroo.

Sign up to try the newest flavors in the Taste Testing Kitchen where small batches are made up following the dreams of the jerky chefs. Taste testers not only get a crack at the flavor drops but also have the opportunity to give their feedback on what might be the next mouthwatering hit.

119 E Reno Ave., 877-975-3759
jerky.com

CHECK OUT MORE OF OKLAHOMA'S OWN JERKY

Uptown Jerky Co.
2418 N Robinson Ave., 405-551-5166
uptownjerky.com

Dusty's Real Beef Jerky
628 SE 82nd St., 855-338-7897
dustysbeefjerky.com

The GOAT Beef Jerky Company
400 S Vermont Ave., Ste. 127, 405-604-4638

START FEELING JOLLY
AT NORTH POLE CITY

There may be days over 100 degrees in OKC in September, but Christmas comes early thanks to North Pole City. Originally "The Christmas Shop" in the early 1980s, David Green's dream of Christmas magic has grown into a true attraction for the city.

The store is a winter wonderland filled with all the boxes, ribbon, nutcrackers, and displays fitting to be seen in an old-fashioned Christmas. They have something for everyone, whether extra-long strings of LED lights or handcrafted glass ornaments. Anything you could need, whether a huge nutcracker or one to fit the mantelpiece, a tabletop ceramic, or an enormous artificial tree. They stock top-of-the-tree decorations from some of the best names in Christmas, like Ino Schaller and Poland's Huras Family. Even if you don't know what you need yet, come in to take a peek . . . it's safer than peeking at your presents!

4201 S I-44 Service Rd., 405-685-6635
northpolecity.com

TIP

North Pole City is open September to January, so come early to feel festive in the fall or come in after the holidays to plan for next year.

REVISIT THE PAST
AT DECADES REVISITED, A VINTAGE MALL

Step into a world of nostalgia at Decades Revisited, a charming vintage mall nestled along the iconic Route 66. This treasure trove is a haven for enthusiasts of all things retro, boasting an eclectic collection of vintage furniture, mid-century modern pieces, repurposed antiques, and an array of quirky items that redefine the term "junk." Wander through a constantly evolving space where the inventory changes daily, ensuring every visit is a unique experience. Featuring everything from timeless classics to hidden gems, Decades Revisited is a haven for collectors and casual shoppers alike. Whether you're a seasoned vintage aficionado or just looking for a distinctive piece to add character to your home, with 9,000 square feet of floor space, Decades Revisited promises a delightful journey through the decades.

3639 NW 39th St., 405-601-6800
decadesrevisited.com

HANG OUT AND SHOP
AT SAILOR & THE DOCK

Is it a bar? Is it a small-shop mall? Is it an event venue? Yes!

Sailor & the Dock is an experience all its own. The reclaimed sailboat, revitalized into a bar, makes it a fun place to hang out, but that's only the anchor for its world. Local small businesses come together to surround the bar with everything someone could want: a low-waste living store, a chic bookshop, a vintage clothing store, and more. All that shopping making you hungry? Grab a bite at the farm-to-table café, which has coffee good enough to be its own destination.

Then come the events. Its space offers open mics, indoor sailing lessons, retro movies, trivia, and endless opportunities for socializing. People like it so much they rent it out for themselves.

It was all done as an eco-conscious feat by renovating a century-old warehouse into something altogether new and beneficial for the city.

617 W Sheridan Ave., 405-237-5984
sailorandthedock.com

SPIN A NEW RECORD
AT OKC'S VINYL SHOPS

Sometimes media devices like VCRs and laser discs fade away with time, but vinyl records have defied all the odds in becoming many music lovers' top choice. There's just something about the way analog audio captures a nuance and depth to the music that a streamlined, perfected digital format can never quite do. As the heart of the state, we have some of the coolest spots around where you can dig to find what you'll dig next.

Guestroom stands as perhaps the best known, still rocking the town with its own presses for records of Oklahoma artists. Trolley Stop Record Shop, situated in the acoustically rich space of the old Penn Theater, specializes in vintage records and hosts shows.

1212 N Pennsylvania Ave., 405-208-8833

TIP

Monkey Feet Music, housed in a law office building, boasts an eclectic collection. Alley Records, a passion project, serves as a diverse haven for music enthusiasts, embracing a wide array of genres.

Guestroom Records
3701 N Western Ave., 405-601-3859

Monkey Feet Music
3801 N Classen Blvd., 405-628-9323

Alley Records
918 1/2 W Britton Rd., 405-778-9026

The Soundbar
712B N Broadway Ave, 405-404-9832
thesoundbarokc.com

Scissortail Park, courtesy of Dennis Spielman

ACTIVITIES
BY SEASON

SPRING

SUMMER

FALL

WINTER

Asian Night Market Military Park, courtesy of Jeff Provine

Flamingo Tiki, courtesy of Dennis Spielman

SUGGESTED ITINERARIES

DATE NIGHT

BUDGET FRIENDLY

FOR THE KIDS

THRILL SEEKERS

MUSEUM CRAWL

DOG FRIENDLY

Blue Sage Studios, courtesy of Dennis Spielman

INDEX